IAN GOUGE

PUNCTUATIONS FROM HISTORY

First published in paperback format by
Coverstory books, 2018

ISBN 978-1-9997840-3-4

Copyright © Ian Gouge 2018

The right of Ian Gouge to be identified as the author of this work has been asserted by them in accordance with the Copyright, Designs and Patents Act 1988.

All characters and events in this publication. other than those clearly in the public domain, are fictitious and any resemblance to real persons, living or dead, is purely coincidental.

All rights reserved.

No part of this publication may be reproduced, circulated, stored in a system from which it can be retrieved, or transmitted in any form without the prior permission in writing of the publisher.

www.coverstorybooks.com

Other Books by Ian Gouge

Novels and Novellas

Mirrors - Paperback, 2017; Kindle, 2015

Losing Moby Dick and Other Stories - Coverstory books, 2017

Losing Moby Dick - Kindle 2015

Writing to Gisella - Kindle 2015

Riding the Escalators - Kindle 2015

The Big Frog Theory - Paperback, 2017; Kindle, 2012

Short Stories

Secrets & Wisdom - Coverstory books, 2017

Poetry

Human Archaeology - Paperback, 2017

Collected Poems (1979-2016) - Paperback, 2017

Second Sight - Kindle, 2013

Walking Thru Fire - Kindle 2012

Table of Contents

I

Punctuations from History 9
The Refugee Dance 13
The Search for Proof 14
Theft 16
The Stone Circle 17
End of an Ice Age 19
The Catch 20
Changing Faces 21
Among the Ruins 27
Weather Forecast 29

II

The Pennines - Early Winter 33
Suburbia 34
Delta 35
Cocktails in the Infinity Pool 36
Sandstorm 37
On Finding Themselves In Darkness 38
Coast 39
Islanders 41
The Disenfranchised 42
The Psychologists 43
Making The Climb 44
Envy 45
Fragments 46
The Light of Our Lives 48
Sounds of the House 49
Public Image 53
Fruit-crate Prophet 54
Unearthing 55
Ambition 56

III

Unauthorised Biography 59
Reflection in a Cracked Mirror 60
Lost 61
The Wanting 62
Curse 63
Late to the Marquee 64
Obsession 65
Ninety-nine Percent 66
Greybeard's Lament 67
The Reticence of Evolution 69
Slow-motion Apocalypse 70
The Holly Leaf 71
Autumn 72
Elemental 73
Driving Home for Christmas 75
Trapped by the Tides 76
Veritas 78
The Fallacy 79
Minutes 80

IV

Contextual Introduction to the Poems 83

I

Punctuations from History

i

"The loop shares a kinship with
a remnant from the brewhouse"

        scarred by tawny rust
                the imprints of a Cooper's fingertips
                      the aura of oak and hops

        caught in a shaft of sunlight
        a glint from history
        as if illuminated dust might rearrange itself
        to turn back time
                to bring back echoes from the forge
                      the headiness of ale
        come full circle
        even as the loop leans unused
                              unwanted
                forgotten against the ruined walls

ii

"A chair cut in half but still standing
damaged, halved, surviving"

        split
        cleft asunder
        mimicking past usefulness and
        presenting a fractured image of itself
                nonchalant
                as if nothing had happened
                as if it had always been thus

        a chair that is not a chair
        a thing that is not a thing
              become image
                    or parody
        disguised to look like itself
                        or how it was

        we nod at the deception
        and recognise in the once-chair
        a mirror of ourselves
        and how we were
              or how we are now
                      or how we might yet be

iii
"In sympathy with the plight of Saints
a pilgrimage full of geographical detail"

        factual is not spiritual
        full of instruction and order
        of where, or when, or how
              to march
              to eat
              to rest

        the journey is a test
        in fulfilling the rules
                of adherence

        orienteering without passion
        collecting the badge
              the certificate of completion

        this is about trophy
                not selflessness
        a tick on a bucket list
                not self-discovery
        a closure
                not an awakening

iv
"Elongated and tailored to the topography
a spirit level unable to find equilibrium"

    disproving the feeling
        that you are on even ground
    the power of the bubble holds sway
    a demonstration of air
        and gravity
            and forces beyond our comprehension

    adjusting
        re-sighting
            we hope for another outcome
            as if there must be a way
            to disprove this reality

    suffocated
        unable to escape
            we resign ourselves
            to the uncertainty of imbalance
            and cast the level
                into the tilting skip

v
"The markers of space around language

an ever-present sign of life"

    there is energy in the void
        and unseen potential

scrabbling in the mottled dark
with inadequate instruments
we endeavour to excavate
    our uneven treasures
hoping when they are cleaned
    polished to a new and burnished hue
they reveal something undiscovered
    - or at least unseen in our lifetime

have you noticed how beyond
Archaeologists' veneer of romance
    their clothes are shabby
    and their skin scarred
    like the earth in which they dig?

The Refugee Dance

They thought their provenance
        descended from settlers
would be a guarantee of status,

instead they subsist in
        a dusty hive of huts
corralled in a field

far from the image of Paradise.
        The soldiers' coming found them
fearing for their lives,

the gun-waving Captain
        flashing a smile
and asking the women to dance.

Later, when they had gone,
        a neighbour lamented
the wave of brutality

and told the story of how
        she had found the man-child,
a bullet in his back.

The Search for Proof

It was the sign of a Craftsman,
        dirtying his hands indoors, tidying things up.
Outside, when work was done,
        looking out across the sprawl of walls,
a mosaic of pale terracotta beyond which
        a suffering crowd had gathered.
Calm, he welcomed questions with bemused patience
        still coming to terms with his bestowed profile,
cosmopolitan champion of social justice.

Centuries later, desperation shouts
        the odds for unearthing evidence:
decaying cedar beams elaborately carved,
        buried by decades of candle soot;
a fishing smack exposed at low tide, its skeleton
        repeatedly patched and repaired.
Archaeology gives life to tradition,
        faint footprints ever more distinct.

People who proclaim to know better,
        argue physical evidence is too elusive
and the stained-glass story is but an invention
        fitting a pre-ordained scenario,
its polished surface endlessly rubbed over time.

Ultimately overwhelmed by questions of history,
        the scholar's quest is of little consequence;
speculation shares crowded shelves with measuring reels
        and sepia-tinted, frayed-edge photographs
of darkened nooks etched with reliquary and graffiti.
        Undaunted, they search for shards from a single life,

for a brief and spectacular moment of exposure;
      they dig for the real man hiding below the surface,
hoping for a heel bone driven through with an iron nail.

Theft

Their faces were stolen in 1828
when stained glass lead outweighed
the souls of people.
Empty spaces now stare back,
blank are the ovals that leave no clue
to the characters of Saints who
unknowing made the sacrifice.

Two centuries of loss are commemorated
by collages in a sculpture exhibition;
shadows and whispers from the past
and a brief note in the simple catalogue:
"their faces were stolen in 1828".

seen in Haddon Hall, Derbyshire, UK [13th August, 2017]

The Stone Circle

They would have left tracks,
scars rough hewn in the moor's skin
as they dragged their burden up,
up from some long-forgotten quarry
now boulder-strewn and green grown over.
Where you walk now
- a signposted trail marched into dry sand -
might once have been the course
of the standing stones you seek.
Who can say?
And the pagan voices - shouts of pain,
of orders, of urgings to pull harder -
are feint in the echoes of modern parents who
coax or admonish, and who promise
"not far to go now".
Was it worth it for them,
after all that effort,
the nine stones standing in a perfect circle,
perfectly separated one from the other?
What magic was satisfied
in the completion of their task?
Perhaps they encouraged the legend
of dancers turned to stone for heresy;
perhaps they needed some mystery, some danger,
in order to invest their efforts
with a meaning and portent that would out-live them.
People recline against the midget stones,
or lie between them; or stepping up,
make the small and unspectacular leap
back to the flat grassed clearing.
Across the scrub, voices rise from camp-fire singing,

and smoke drifts skywards
from instant barbecues and processed meat.
The ancient stones remain a meeting place of sorts
timeless in that one sense at least
even if its architects have long since
themselves returned to the earth.

End of an Ice Age

There is no place for us on our ancestral lands.
Lines -
      road
           rail
                  pipe
                        power
- cut across our heritage and our migration routes.
It is too far to go around, and many
are too weak for the long journey
even where crossing is expedient and safe.

As we head disconsolately south,
swells of tundra close north behind us and
the midnight sun fills less the icy surface of the lakes;
somewhere nearby humming refrigeration units
strive to keep the weakening ground frozen.

We dream of being where the landscape settles
into familiar shapes and colours,
where we can take our time ice-fishing,
and where we truly know ourselves.

The Catch

An oar bangs against the hull
as idle fishermen lounge in the boat laughing.
Pulling a meagre catch from depleted waters
was the jolt that rocked them
into observation of a self-imposed ban.

Hungry families moving from camp to camp
led to a lone-cowboy culture,
desperation in those now turned traitor
and paid to watch for poachers.

Long after, the cycle of history may prove
there's time for detachment and
always space to bring back a community.

Undaunted, life rebounds within its borders
even as the inky black ocean slaps again at the sand.

Changing Faces

i. The Mask

Look.
A largely forgotten cultural artefact
fundamental to notions of identity,
to effacement, disguise and the resonance
of hiding motivation and concealing truth,
the mask has greater significance
than would first appear,
its duality revealing the way
the world is viewed by both
wearer and audience,
the change into some other being
an absolute separation
of the everyday self.

Complexity and subtlety of meaning
are integral parts of a masquerade,
an event, a performance;
the entire ensemble
implicit in cunning trickery,
the suspension of disbelief
transforming identity completely.

Only those who were privileged
had the right to own ancestral masks,
could afford the impersonation of character
to create an indeterminate nature
at the boundaries of interaction between
truth and falsehood,

the human and the spiritual,
the living and the dead.
Masks inhabited by forefathers,
shadows of their former selves,
offered the ideal of an ancestral return.

Masks, it could be said, carry memory.

Metaphors for the moments of change
observed behind glass-fronted cabinets
and reduced to their sculptural essentials,
masks in museums stripped of their
extra-human dimension and idealised identity
are just a display of dead things.

ii Mask of a Young Woman

Whitened with eggshell,
hair and feathers delicately painted on;
the false eyebrows high on the forehead
and the blackened teeth were
fashionable cosmetic styles for over a thousand years.

Theatre masks provided opportunity for expression,
standard masks for different dramas
where subtle changes of expression were honed
by the way in which the head was turned.

iii In the Form of a Wolf

Clan headdresses were worn in feasts by native peoples,
headdresses of cedar bark and goat wool,
regalia to celebrate life-cycle events.

A member of the eagle clan
came across a wolf smiling,
something stuck between his teeth.
The mask removed, the wolf disappeared
only to reappear again in a dream.

Regalia was passed down the female line.

iv Mummy Mask

A depiction of the head and chest
was worn outside the shroud
to act as a substitute for the head
should it become lost;
the spirit could leave the confines of a tomb
and when returning recognise its host.

Created from layers of wet linen
moulded over a thin outer skin,
mummy masks were rarely portraits,
their backs decorated with a row of deities
and seven short columns of near intelligible hieroglyphs.

v Death Mask of Oliver Cromwell

Used as a model for posthumous portraits
here was a permanent record of the way he looked
captured before the features started to fail
(his wart succumbed to the embalming fluid!).

Later his body was exhumed
and his real head displayed on a pole
to be finally buried in Cambridge in the 1960s
300 years after he died.

Subsequently the Death Mask was sold many times.

vi Mask of a Demon

In Life, a significant event
was an attack by
one of the eighteen disease demons.
A primitive antibody
used in healing rituals,
the most powerful of cures was a masked performance
of both dramatic moments and comedy.

vii Wooden Face Mask

Distended cheeks were associated with the city,
the ruler blowing blessings onto his people.

> [And the meaning today?
> Being bloated, or the expulsion of air in relief,
> as if to say "I got away with that one"...]

viii Wooden Helmet Mask

Representative of an ideal of female beauty:
glossy skin,
small facial features,
folds of fat at the neck.

During initiation girls were kept in check
and masks used to regulate female behaviour.

Apart from this exception
masking traditions were
activities otherwise limited to males.

ix *Stone Funerary Mask*

Sculpted in a greenish stone
selected for its symbolic value,
these were heavy masks
not intended to be worn
but rather mounted on a wooden armature
and dressed with elaborate costumes.

Inheriting subtle elements
from earlier traditions,
the features of this funerary mask
and the symmetry in its surface
echoed rigid architectural canons
and public mythologies of the ceremonial.

x *Cavalry Sports Helmet*

Resplendent,
the richly-decorated equipment
- beaten brass shining golden yellow
embossed with battle scenes -
was worn on cavalry sports events,
flamboyant displays involving complex manoeuvres.

The youthful lively faces of the soldiers
a contrast to the chilling, immobile faces of the masks.

xi *Yam Mask*

Decorated yams were
exchanged between men
and displayed publicly,

the ancestral spirits represented
feted with offerings and decorations
to seek spiritual well-being and
survival in a single cosmology.

Among the Ruins

You step over hinge-torn twisted gates
hanging from fragile metal threads,
one dented by a gate-post eagle
that unexpectedly flew to ground
in the unexpected storm.
Reaching the now-rutted drive, you see
trimmed edges blurred by unchecked leaves
free to sit in gullies, gutters, the shallow
depressions of long-grassed verges,
free to rot to mulch.
Beyond the elegant curve,
forlorn hedges, box that has lost its shape,
swans and peacocks now deformed
by renegade and unruly spurs
protruding from all angles;
and then, that first vista of the house
still resplendent from this distance.
Closer, treading with care
to avoid unbroken icy puddles,
you notice those first-floor window panes,
four by three, all shattered;
someone's target practice.
And there, and there too, glass gone,
protection breached for the rooms beyond.
The fractured remains of a chimney pot;
the entrance, once boastful and proud,
speaking eloquently in slime green and white.
Pausing, you brush leaves and muck
with the back of your gloved hand
from the small stone wall,
then ease yourself down with a sigh,

resting your stick upright at your side,
pulling the hat from your hairless head,
loosening your scarf.
Then closing your eyes, you fix the gate,
sweep the drive, get Jim from the village
to re-pane the broken windows;
and there's faithful Jock,
hard at work with the clippers
making the peacocks fit to sing again.
And you race down the drive once more
- "First one to the gate's the winner!" -
with Douglas and Victoria;
Douglas always winning, Victoria always last
no matter the head start she had!
You can hear their laughter in the wind
and their chatter in the whipped-up leaves,
but you hear it now alone.

Weather Forecast

The temperature falls and heavy mottled clouds
lacking the playfulness of summer
skim above my head and threaten to envelop me
in some apocalyptic deluge.
Looking at the skies, I search for the break,
the glimmer of hope heralded by a schism of blue
that the sun will return to vanquish a grey
which seems to dominate the world.

From somewhere comes an antique image
of a young boy bent to a task
as if from a black-and-white photograph
glimpsed through the frost of almost-opaque glass.
His hand is raised in mid-operation
as if about to apply the finishing touch,
the final piece, concentration evident
despite the blurring of his outline.
He is poised on the brink of achievement
and I wonder who he is, his silhouette
the tyranny of the past and the echo of someone
I might once have been.

Raising an inadequate collar against the urgent wind
I recall a past encounter
as if such occupation might protect me
like an umbrella against the rain that must surely come.
He had been much like me,
but not a man mirror-looking;
one with a now-lost geography about him
that required no map or compass
to set direction or find his way.

His step had been confident,
unencumbered by concerns about weather;
the walk of a man who could see where he was headed,
travelling a path without obstruction.
There were challenges of course;
the scrapes of bramble when the path narrowed,
the labouring when it climbed,
a need to tread with care when it fell away
skirting a precipice that these days would bring fear.
I envy him and try to imagine walking in his shoes,
enjoying the lightness of step and striving to embrace
his obliviousness to its blessing.
I lost him somewhere, my concentration stolen,
a gate, or a misplaced step and the perils of footfall.
Perhaps there had been a fork in the way,
a divergence that I missed and, not looking back,
he simply walked away from me.
I always assumed that he was still ahead,
around the next corner, waiting for me there.
Abandoned, he never was.

An age has passed since then,
a separate journeying that leaves me here
unprotected against the rain, longing for summer -
and haunted by the mottled image
of a black-and-white boy.

II

The Pennines - Early Winter

The dusted snow lay as if a Breughel
(Elder or Younger) had breezed by,
brush and titanium white in hand,
and treated the landscape to a wash of their talents.
Tufts of rough moor grass poked their fibrous heads
into the stiff northern wind,
clumps of brown punctuating the mucky white
as if some migratory flock had invisibly done its business
then moved on elsewhere.
The watery light made the snow retreat a little,
its battle with the bitter wind
adjudicated to a draw.
No doubt they will go at it again tomorrow
though the snow (by Breughel or not)
may mount another raid under darkness' covers.
There is a balance between the elements even so,
as if the hills, the frozen fronds,
the black-dark clumps of northern pine
have discovered an accord,
a settlement negotiated elsewhere,
a treaty of simple clauses allowing for all eventualities
and rendering the actions of man laughably irrelevant.
Across the field, a dry stone wall
begs repair, as if in those fallen stones
a barrier has been breached and consequence threatened.
But it is illusion. The scrub, the snow, the rocks,
the incessant trilling of the stream still holds sway,
a panoply over which not even
the oldest Master can exert influence.

Suburbia

Despite their manicured accuracy,
front lawns are sun-scorched, hosepipe-banned
in a summer unseasonably hot;
yet vast stretches of fettered green
seem to have been forgotten by time,
a compendium of open spaces
drafted in straight from central casting.
In an unspoken way,
camouflaged behind each High Street glance,
everything narrows to a nervous point,
an exam set of moral questions asking
if quality of existence is a matter of human whim.
Perhaps there is never-ending irony
lying beyond our incomprehension, and
the feeling that it should have been enough
to have lived in the suburbs.

Delta

North beyond the low plains of reeds
and the whiteness of precipitated salt,
meaningful presence is sparse.
Beyond the trill of crickets
a single tethered donkey grazes
on an ever-changing paisley carpet.

Coming from two countries away
like blossom pressed onto the landscape,
petals of silvery water splay out,
its veins seep into tributaries
and sink invisibly into the sands,
the draining away of lifeblood.

Cocktails in the Infinity Pool

Singapore wears her skirts high above the knee,
proud of her slim and tanned thighs.
Her shopping malls mesmerise,
their glimmer, gold and glitz, veneer-deep,
a film of tropical sweat glistening
on a body we all desire.

Across a polished sky, a grey mass
threatens to unload its burden;
rain that will sing as it bounces off
swimming pools and Ferraris,
trapping you where you stand
or forcing you indoors,
in to air-conditioned boutiques,
French pastries, Italian coffee and
faux New York sidewalks.

And yet.
There is history here if you care to look,
if you bother to make the journey out to Kranji
or see Changi as more than just a destination
for departures and duty-free;
long hauls of another kind are buried
not so far beneath the surface.
Perhaps it is apt that her history
is a precious metal to be stroked not scratched,
to be caressed by cotton gloves
and melancholic remembrance
- and then forgotten,
conquered by expeditions to Channel, Louis Vuitton,
and cocktails in the infinity pool.

Sandstorm

It is impossible to ignore the proximity of the sea,
how it made a natural harbour,
and the reason the city exists.

Absorbed by an unspoken need
to mould something beyond that naturally given,
invention destroyed the town's ancient enterprise;
and looking suddenly inwards,
developers carved up the land and raced
unrestricted into an audacity obsessed with glittering visions
of a skyline of architectural wonders
disproving that most enduring mirage:
a golden city rising from the sands.

It is impossible to ignore the proximity of the sea
and its ever-more crucial role in prolonging
the lives of those who chase an ever-expanding footprint.

On Finding Themselves In Darkness

On finding themselves in darkness
they tried to speak eloquently of the stars
and conveyed surprise at their number,
brightness, brilliance,
>   or that they were there at all.

It was a lesson in the inadequacy of language
watching them struggle to portray
the mix of wonder and awe that probably
chased their breath away
>   and left them smaller than before.

They should lay in a hammock
loose-strung between two acacia trees
and stare upwards from the African scrub
where pollution of the sky cowers
>   beyond the furthest horizon.

They should merge that sense of the infinite
with the loneliness of being cast
adrift in thousands of unvarnished acres
accompanied by barks and howls and sounds
>   beyond your comprehension.

This indigo vastness is close-coupled
with a finite that can only shrink,
with a worthlessness that can only grow,
with a pulse that is suddenly becalmed
>   even as the heart skips a little.

Coast

Trace around its outline with great care,
there is danger as well as beauty there.
Go slowly, cautiously;
try to picture postcard scenes
of secluded coves, a deserted beach,
the caves where smugglers hid
and waited for the tide to reach.
Pause again where once upon a kid
you ate fish and chips with Gran,
or cream fruit scones with Auntie Fran;
or walking that neglected path,
held hands with Ruth's sister, Kath.
Crab fishing from the pier!
Or chasing pollock with a plastic reel;
a Fair, a Carousel, the Dodgems' cheer,
the Candy-floss's sickly smell,
screaming at the Waltzer's spell;
a litany of buckets, spades,
vampires, Goths, Sunday parades,
yachts, hovercraft, Bank Holiday swathes
of tourists, row boats, crazy golf,
and over-flowing ice cream sundaes.
You touched the sea more than you knew.
Retracing steam to Dartmouth,
the winding roads to Lyme, St. Ives;
coach trips near and far,
Saltburn's red funicular;
Blackpool's lights, Brighton's sights,
Bournemouth nights, and Whitby frights;
a multicoloured film of wooden huts,
of dunes and skimming stones,

sandcastles fighting incoming tides;
of grit in shoes when walking home,
of dodging dog shit, the ends of fags,
of wading in the freezing drink
which made your little willie shrink!
Trace your finger round the coast with care;
where land meets sea, your history is there.

Islanders

They have a special aura, those
                fine-tuned to life on the harsh isles.
Standing on a cliff, they watch
                the sea retreat in a white flag of foam,
their remoteness permitting them to
                live as much in myth as on a map.
Yet like us, they boast no divine insight,
                and try to see what the future will hold
even as we imagine them
                striding through dim highland forests
and living contented lives
                in a landscape without concrete.

The Disenfranchised

Laboratory experiments rumble on
        measuring the progress of individuals
        bereft of almost every resource.
White-coated, we watch them
        mature into voracious consumers whose
        hunger and poverty are not abstract threats.
Unwanted and unemployed, they are
        used to living marginal lives beset
        by constant conversations on their needs:
what others have and what they covet is
        a fragmented patchwork of promise
        glinting when the sun shines.
Lacking sophisticated mechanisms
        many defend themselves naturally,
        their ambitions for the future
a white-knuckle ride on a torrent of predictions;
        different perspectives and common goals
        exposed in black-and-white studies
clip-board-captured in shallow generic portraits.

The Psychologists

They spend their days in intimate study
        of people they do not know,
of Outsiders who might need their help,
        who face into a cacophonous mess
where grief and hope are huddled together
        wedged into the darkest corner
of something they can neither touch nor define.

Peering at them through microscopes
        made from language and gesture,
theirs is a drawn out process of watching,
        of looking for hidden clues.

It is not a mortal assault on the majority
        yet our ignorance sees it so;
from their vivid and theoretical engagements
        no-one can accurately tally
the numbers of lives permanently altered
        with the safety mark back in place.

Protected by a holographic shell
        they live through trauma without ill effect,
a self-regulating valve meaning
        only the smallest number are dangerous.

Making The Climb

In the solitude of a breathless pause
he surveys the next slab of granite,
mapping the likely traverse
and clinging to an unwavering commitment
against the most difficult part:
knowing there is certain death should he lose his grip.

"People who climb cliffs unharnessed are idiots!"

Away from this lens-sharp quiet,
the capital seems a foreign country;
a pulsing mass of thousands where
poverty and isolation means misery for many.
It is a mystery to wide-ranging adventurers like him.

His search for portals into a separate reality
is a rugged and never-ending two-way trek
that alternates between light and dark;
and when the magic begins to fade away
he can be consumed by a sudden
and sometimes wrathful energy.

"Children don't value culture!"

Yet how can they?
He knows they have never led the harvest,
never seen the elevation of the flowers -
that crescent-shaped carpet of brilliance! -
nor worn a vest made from stinging nettles
as they search for something invisible in the air.

Envy

They stand beside us like shadows
we would love to cast, their flagstone patterns
images we would mimic.
Existing here yet pursuing different strategies,
we love them for their fight, transfixed
by the bloody grimace we trace upon them.
Yet perversely, they are not against peace;
distinguished from our less-rare cousins
by the potential to grow,
their consistent harvest over the years
not measurable in precise figures.
Seeming to fill the whole sky,
we marvelled at what they built
and lost ourselves in mythical superlatives.

>   Ashamed,
>   afraid of being the Loser,
>   we turn, hoping to have gone unnoticed,
>   and leave our hopes to rust away.

Fragments

The uneven planes of a shattered mirror.
        A conversation only partly overheard.
                The remnants of a broken plate.

Images lost or ill-defined
marry shapes and edges for
memory's trial, a virtual jigsaw.

        Was it really sunny that day?
        Was the train on time or late?
        Did I plan it all so well,
        or did I leave it all to fate?

Seven years' bad luck?
        An inflection missed?
                Did that plate escape wet hands?

The lure of flawless hindsight,
to know if - spoken, thrown in anger -
outcomes betray how we feel.

        Did it rain ceaselessly,
        closing all the sea-front stalls
        as we, close-coupled in a shelter,
        watched waves assault the sea-front walls?

Here is the mark of absence where it hung.
        The phone has gone; the line is dead.
                Dust balls circle the once-swept floor.

We close our eyes to open our minds,

sifting through the fragments
for the missing piece.

> *Was sea-fret the reason*
> *I lost you on that sea-front day?*
> *Or were there other clues - a mirror, a plate -*
> *as to why you went away?*

The Light of Our Lives

We have a jar in our bedroom
where we keep the fragment
that fell from the sky and
buried itself in the garden the day
we moved into our new house.
Some days the shard would glow
and the jar illuminate
with an impossible light,
and if we removed the lid
the light escaped and our world
and our lives became
just a little more wonderful.
We were blessed when it landed.

But recently the glow is more reticent;
our rock is alive less frequently,
and so it has become harder to top-up
our lives from this astral gift
and we are forced to carry on
as if it never arrived,
as if we were just like other people.
Each evening before bed
I check the jar, ever-hoping;
wishing once again to be able to let
a fraction of the brilliance escape.
But it is always dark these days
and when the lights are off
our bedroom is as black as the sky.

Sounds of the House

i - Footfall

>There's an echo from the stairs;
>clipped tread on parquet floor;
>stilettos trotting in the hall.

Through sound-porous brick, a life that is not mine.
The hasty climb up uncarpeted stairs -
to where? And what to do when she gets there?

It was late when she returned.
I imagine her, unstable on thin red heels,
out with the girls, too many gins,
Dutch Courage fuelling her search
since unexpectedly he left.

I may not see her in the morning,
laid low by a thumping head
or sickness and self-promise, "never again".

ii - Doors

>The slamming from the porch;
>our Postie dropping mail;
>the turning of a stubborn lock.

How welcome a delivery was that?
Ray's a friendly soul, a ready wit,
always with a word about
inclemency or the cost of petrol.
Nothing for me today (this Valentine's)
but at least one for her, I know.

Was that not enough?
Did she slam the door, lock herself in,
because she wanted, needed more?
Or because there wasn't one from 'him'?

iii - Kitchen Clatter

        The clash of copper pots and pans;
          an unplanned smash of plates;
        cutlery spilling from the drawers.

It brokered silence.
From cacophony to nothing, then later
him walking down the path
suitcase in hand.
No backward glance.

I wonder what she broke,
or what she threw.
I've seen signs of temper, witnessed nothing
- until the moment their kitchen exploded
through *my* kitchen wall.

In the aftermath, the apologetic echo
in the sweeping of broken pieces,
the damage done.

iv - Singing

        A rusty bathroom baritone;
         a flawed operatic aria;
      the belted off-key Number One.

I miss nothing of him.
He used to sing sometimes, badly.

I imagine him in the shower,
satisfied after sex, thinking he's Timberlake;
a broken, unreliable timbre
with dodgy notes at both range-ends.
I never envied him his voice
only his reason for singing.

v - Manufactured Voices
>Modern music's thumping bass;
>a TV advert's jingle;
>the radio's dull dialogue drone.

The music she likes surprises me.
Having imagined a different playlist
to accompany her life,
this heavy beat feels out of kilter,
its vibration through my feet.

She plays her TV too loud
and I can tell the shows she likes.
Occasionally, radio; news updates, little more.
A pause between the main events.

vi - Conversation
>A background hum of dialogue;
>the half-empty telephone call;
>the sharpness of a sudden shout.

When she has friends round
they stay camped in the kitchen.
The wall is thicker here perhaps,
their voices indistinct, almost silent,
punctuated by a laugh, a shout

- what *was* all that about?!

Her phone is in the hall.
I hear her one-sided calls.
On the other end, is it him?
Seeking reconciliation?
Or her, beyond humiliation?

Public Image

He tried to remember
a time before cameras were present,
an unparalleled bliss bequeathed from
a period of solitude and discovery,
a time when language was everything
and he recorded observations by name.

Oblivious to their deceptions, he missed
their unspoken desire to generate
an intimate view at a pivotal time,
their spending months trying to get
close enough to be in camera range.

Trapped, they started checking off the boxes,
a tick-list of illusions, footage of him
appearing to be doing research against
a patently unscientific background narration.
Their funding hinged on his willingness to be glamourised,
acceptance of the duality of the public image being crafted;
and all the while they obscured from him
the myth they were creating in their own minds.
The film was a milestone in his emergence as a public figure
igniting what became a legendary career
that compromised all his prevailing beliefs.

Knowing that over time he would be forgotten,
he started to save for an ocean passage
and dreamed of giving a whole speech whose destiny
was not to lie shredded on a cutting room floor.

Fruit-crate Prophet

Navigating the alchemy of human geography
and failing in the search for pure gold,
he discovers pleasure, purpose and pride,
three strands that braid together
to offer a compact meaning for a life
where time is described as 'flow'
and people report feeling emotions
that nudge them into singular behaviours.

Guided by enlightened leaders,
colonial institutions introduce policies
that might easily translate into solutions
to catch diseases before they erupt,
to manage the price of produce;
the elegant mix of Private and Public,
an apt metaphor for a society trying to
sketch out the end of a roughly-defined path.

Standing on a rustic wooden plinth
he is a fixture at the weekly market;
living among like-minded people,
on the weekends he worships God.
He has a gift for defusing tension,
for questioning the unquestioned;
and when challenged he quotes
his unrelenting mantra,
"We have a jewel to preserve".

Unearthing

running along the leading edge
        of a benevolent weather-front
they might soar on friendly thermals
        across oceans for days at a time
seeking the common name given to the first
        uninhabited paradise

in a windowless storage room
        enclosed in a bunker of a building
preserved by some quirk of geology
        popular notions still keep alive
an unshakeable belief that combining
        the mathematical with the hands-on
can lead you to the Grail
        the mother lode of modern discovery

facing the sad lot of the perennially typecast
        you need to be an optimist
to decipher the nuances of life
        to conjure up forgotten worlds
when facing a spirit of muted hostility
        permanently hooked on the eradication of romance

Ambition

What little light there is,
                diffused through a grey fog,
is draped inadequately over the landscape.

Emerging suddenly from the gloom
                and with no accurate maps to guide them,
we watch them running clumsily around
                trying to find where all the treasure's hid,
emotions evaporating on perpetual boil.

In this environment
                you cannot feign passion.
Facing the ever-present threat of being
                stunned by disappointment or caught
in a slow-motion train wreck,
                nerves fray at the edge.
You have to be sure of your desire.

Unauthorised Biography

There are rivers that flow
subterranean through people's lives,
mythological, impossible for navigation.
Yet lured by the glory of discovery,
an expedition is commissioned
to capture the interest of the public body;
the Life-Story, an ideal proxy battleground to
camouflage and disrupt the facts.

Suddenly dissected overnight,
their sense of being trap-caught
is mostly met with fatalism,
knowing that foresight
was an unrealistic expectation
when faced with others' imperatives
that change from week to week.

The hardback confluence of their lives
now insulated with another currency
is become a course not for revisiting;
the attempts at spiritual enrichment
devoid of any higher motivation
beyond the vacuous and sensational.

Reflection in a Cracked Mirror

I know the Earth in an intimate way,
        our addiction to time and
the systems that keep us alive.

Today is taken up with one long task:
        the looking back to see where we failed.
And so I try to put myself in their place,

to re-learn that doubt is worse than hunger,
        is the offspring of the myopic,
is a fatal threat the closer it gets.

Life is not haphazard,
        even if we're blinded by the
stunning contrast from light to dark

where the whole of humanity,
        cast adrift from truth, is
in need of a chance to heal.

We lose each other easily,
        denying our duty, succumbing to the
rhythm marking time for a few short hours.

Lost

There is an emptiness here now
>> bled from the boundaries of our histories
>> to become nothing made visible.

Still, you might wonder what all the fuss is about.

We make excuses, apologies,
>> as if compelled to seek permission
>> for what once was, as if blessing is needed.

Words - like 'once', 'remember',
>> 'missing', 'long ago' - ring alarm bells
>> not for us, but for others;

warnings that we wish to intrude,
>> to overlay our past on their present,
>> to steal a gift, a fragment of after-life.

Best not, eh?

Better not to look at that space -
>> on the shelf, beside us in the bed,
>> inside our shrunken heart -

and keep the void, the vacuum safe.

It is ours alone; better to keep it thus.

The Wanting

In the waiting comes the wanting,
a vacuum we are forced to fill
to avoid the tyranny of silence
and the torture of inactivity.
We submit to the thirst of necessity,
sacrificing steadfastness of course
for the comfort of motion
and the belief we are moving forward
even when our journeying is wanton
or ill-advised or shifting us
ever further from our dreams.

In the wanting comes the waiting,
a stillness we would happily embrace
to avoid the futile and the pointless
and the bullying of time.

Curse

Here is a photo of my heart
from when I had not yet met you.
It is not grey, nor weak,
nor shrivelled to half its size;
now, just space enough left
> to pump blood,
> to force left then right,
> to breathe.

What little there is, is now all mine;
capacity for others, I have none.
A heart devoid of finer things;
a heart with fealty to a Wicked Witch
cauldron-cuffed and spitting bitter words:
"Round about the caldron go:
In the poisoned entrails throw."

> The quote is from "Macbeth" by William Shakespeare, Act IV, scene 1.

Late to the Marquee

I find myself alone at a wake,
a wake for all the lost children.

Someone said I should come and take
take some photographs. But then again

       if there is no-one here to see,
       how should I
               should I strive to capture me?

The wind blows harder and unspent
and unspent shreds ribbons, flowers;

and though it's clear what here was meant,
meaning's ravaged by the speeding hours,

       and so there's nothing here to see
       unless I try
               I try to capture me.

Here's a card that bears a name,
a name that once adorned a place.

'Sit here. Sit here and soft declaim
declaim your history, your life's trace.'

       But if there's no-one here to see
       then forfeit,
               forfeit is my soliloquy.

Obsession

Consumed by reckless generosity
here was a rich kid who loved to party his indulgence;
vanity seeking recognition for his compulsive activities,
oblivious to the snowball rolling downhill
and the inevitability that would see
his addiction, his family, eventually collapse.

Craving and habits can overpower reason and
the processes that underlie desire, pleasure.
Preoccupation urging the fast thrill
is the stimulation that taps into our circuitry;
feeling the fireworks, we fail to see the signals
or recognise our inability to stop.

Advances in science and frustration
promote the mirage of repairing the wiring,
of fixing the faulty chemistry in
our alchemy of learning.
Ultimately changing nothing is no more than
a ham-fisted reboot on a frozen computer.

Myopia is now our evolutionary legacy,
blindly scavenging for the misplaced little gifts
that advertise 'Euphoria is calming'.
Belief in smoke-and-mirrors is dangerous;
like reading tea leaves, its reward
never repays the imagination you invest.

Ninety-nine Percent

We feel suffocated indoors
and so jail-break from our domestic confines
only to encounter simple freestanding
structures dotting the countryside:

large phone booths painted salmon pink
whose faded advertisements reinforce the threat
of being ostracised for not cleaning your own home.
Triggering disgust is the hallmark of our community.

Changing behaviour is never easy when
modern laws are rarely enforced and
prejudice remains the nub of the problem,
ever-victorious in defeating hard-won honour.

Greybeard's Lament

Sitting in the cafe of an up-market super-market
retired couples make intermittent small-talk,
all light rain-jackets, pseudo-fleeces and 'Bags for Life'.
Blending into one,
their faces an amalgam as if from an infant state
where none are different.

But they are.

They have charted their unplanned journeys
through ungovernable seas
like medieval explorers, faces full to the wind,
Captains astride the decks of their ships.

But that is too romantic,
too far-fetched for a damp Tuesday morning
somewhere in the North of England.

Dangerously relaxed with fruit scones,
I avoid the mirror
and slouch deeper into the settee's corner
to practice cultivation.
I strive to be more Pirate than Captain,
feint an illusion to spring, vigour unbridled,
cutlass brandished, steel flashing,
readiness unquestioned.

Eyeing me suspiciously
Doreen clears used plates and cups clatteringly
as if to say
       "Who are you kidding?"

Crumbs and detritus hold us back
as do questions about the weather
and Two-For-One special offers.

Burt Lancaster appears at my side
- or doesn't really as he's unseen by Doreen -
and says
> "Who are you kidding?!
> *I* was the 'Real Deal',
> from here to eternity…
> Or as close as."

The extent of *my* gymnastics
is bounded by the 'i' crossword
and minor triumphs over 'harder' Sudoku.
They're victories of sorts
when sipping tea and eating scones
in a super-market cafe on
a damp Northern Tuesday.

The Reticence of Evolution

Shortly after dawn
                              (like a raid, a raid)
they sneak over the park wall
                              ('Quiet!' someone said)
landing lightly on close-cropped grass
                              (and crouching low)
the forested, mist-shrouded slope
                              ('Move - now!')
tinting the humid air green.

      Each time they venture further
      in their fruitless scouring of the forest
      to have their primal moment.

Struggling for emotional connection
                              ('You have to feel it.')
to document a unique moment
                              ('You have to want it.')
once they took a child hostage
                              ('You have to prize it.')
and drowned in guilt for intruding on another's privacy.

      Thanks to extreme conservation measures
      humanity laps at a boundary
      whose only remaining traces are made mythology.

Slow-motion Apocalypse

We came in search of something new
tired of our figurative existence,
lured by the stories of healers
who claimed they could trace the Origin,
        the myth of the Cascades of Insights.

Apprentices brought my passport
and well-worn tickets
promising a glimpse of another world
captured in camera traps,
        the slow-motion apocalypse unfolding.

Under the influence of the Mother Medicine,
bound in a claustrophobic realm of roots,
darkness rushed at us from the forest,
cathedral-like vaults of shadow
        and glistening orchids made of sound.

The Holly Leaf

It danced into the road in front of me
hopping wildly in the wind,
a rudimentary marionette its strings
pulled by an incompetent puppeteer
drunk on memories of summer.

Black as a silhouette,
it jiggered frantically on the spikes of its leaves
as if tiptoeing over hot coals;
and in its mock panic
(at what, the passing of autumn?)
it seemed to be trying to flag me down,
to get me to stop and offer assistance.

Cocooned in my warm, air-conditioned Audi
I drove on, speedily,
the leaf disappearing between my wheels.

At the insistence of the wind
or possessed by an invisible force
I wonder if it danced for others too
or whether that one leaf was mine alone.

Autumn

The church bells were ringing
their Evensong peel
yet how could you hear them
an invisible wind stealing
the sound away and sending it
cascading across the open fields
like a broken promise?

Elemental

Earth = The Realm of Travelling
>Seduced by the romantic lure of
>crossing the world on foot
>and the sepia-edged glory of
>retracing vanished trails,
>they make rash unplanned decisions,
>pivoting suddenly at sharp angles
>only to find themselves lost,
>marooned in an ocean of grass,
>alone, forlorn and unwanted,
>left like dusty boots beside a dry oasis.
>Helpless against a sandstorm,
>they rock gently in a scorching wind
>as the planet creaks underfoot.

Water = The Flow of History
>How old is this moment?
>Time bleeds like an untended wound
>as modern sophistication decays
>into a replica of medieval stasis.
>And still they search, Explorers trying to
>find loose ends and unravel them,
>trying to live up to their
>self-proclaimed image:
>the ultimate Deal-closers.
>To the earth they are nothing special,
>merely nostalgia tourists.

Fire = The Gift of Light
>From somewhere un-navigated and
>beyond the bounds of time,

an iota of light winks into existence.
Man reframes experience in romance:
ripples like moonlight on water,
the sun setting in a chrome sky.
His myths have angels created from light,
turbaned demons corked inside lamps,
and death re-christened as a journey
through a vast gauntlet of blistering light
- or the light of a gilded era just blinked out.

Air = Insubstantial Interpretation

Shackled to an interminable journey
with the mysteries of Time and Light
flowing radially in all directions,
Explorers discover that things are
invisible until they aren't -
or invisible because they are.
The wilful ignorance behind a search
for the nub of some divine revolution
is distilled to a fading triptych.
Trying in the half-light to spear a licked thread
through the eye of a needle is no more than
a failed attempt to attract a little outside attention.
Waking the impure parts of our erring souls
and hoping for messages of love,
this is the only lasting lesson

Driving Home for Christmas

The fog is marginalised now
stubbornly clinging to the valley floor,
hiding out at the blind bend
where the deceptive river quickly runs
and crochets islands of stones.

Headlights reward us with
a misplaced sense of security,
a false confidence of seeing.
Committed, we push on,
leaving behind a whorl of mist,
memory's vortex eloquently rearranged,
kidding us with pattern and structure
and an omnipresent sense of beauty
if only we dared to look.

Later, struggling with inscriptions
in unvanquished greetings cards,
the things we might have said remain
like undefinable droplets in an ever-changing fog.

Trapped by the Tides

The Harvest Moon woke me
barging through the bedroom window
like a burglar of sleep
thrusting itself against pale walls
and dwarfing the feeble glow
from the electric bedside clock.
Slight-parted curtains exposed
the intruder in all its pock-marked glory,
an unrestrained majesty of peace and menace
sitting implacable in the sky,
confident that its awesome trick
- the pretence of being all light's source -
was carried off so consummately
that none could spot the sleight of hand.

Roused by the clarion
in the deep night silence,
this was my harbinger,
purveyor of secret messages buried in codes of light
and smuggled towards me
across a landscape that seemed frozen in time.
In the field outside nothing stirred
and even the perfect hoot of an owl
spoke to the dexterity of the Trickster.
Sleep having been rustled from me
I abandoned the window to seek refuge
in some other kind of radiance.
Retrieving a pad from a drawer
I scavenged a pen from the jacket
hanging dormant on the door
and wrote

'The Harvest Moon woke me
barging through the bedroom window
like a burglar of sleep'.

Veritas

They should have been
                devoted to the pursuit of truth
but found themselves seduced by
                the ubiquity of lying
and the common pressure
                to inflate their image,
to manufacture a second self,
                deceptions crafted for unjust rewards.
Twisted by this blemish in
                nature and the roots of behaviour,
even if we wanted to, we know
                countering with fact would be in vain
and fail to impede their fleet-footed advance
                towards the apex of a pyramid of untruths.
Devalued and impotent,
                the language we use to navigate
is become compromised and redundant
                as if it were the ultimate capitulation.

The Fallacy

Thwarted by their persistent inability
to unearth like-minded visionaries
some tried desperately to succeed by hustling,
straining to imagine any life other than
one woefully in keeping with the norm,
licensed and painstakingly monitored.

Finding time to recover from early failures,
rebuttals and mistakes already made,
ours is now a stronghold no-one can touch.
Some describe their concepts in video,
others stare mesmerised at words;
together, a nearly unbeatable team.

But in the unnameable darkness,
vast, untapped and needy,
the Big Idea has our measure.
Mocking us for past disappointments,
scathing of our pathetic entrapment attempts,
it glides untouched through more than time and space.

Minutes

If visible, they would be charming,
twinkling-eyed, perfect smiles,
voices so smooth they'd sound
as cream and caramel must.
"Take a seat. Relax!
Put your feet up. Have a drink.
Tea? Coffee?
Something a little stronger?"
They take things from you
when you are at your weakest,
unsuspecting, slightly the worse for wear
having opted for the single malt.
They take things from you
when memories are all you have,
memories you still mistake for dreams;
the past, a midnight masquerade
of an impossible future.

IV

Contextual Introduction to the Poems

Punctuations from History

This poem is based on five "found" fragments taken from the descriptions of pieces in a sculpture exhibition. The fragments themselves are linked only by their relation to the exhibition and their nod to the history within which the sculptures themselves fitted. The poems attempt to unravel the found text, to interpret it and give it context, though without specific reference to the location and time period within which the exhibition was staged. Whilst this could have been offered, it would undermine a poem in which part of its heartbeat derives from the tension between fragment and poetic interpretation.

In examining and 're-imaging' the fragments themselves, the poems also attempt to suggest additional import, trying to draw out of the abstract yet another layer of meaning. So #1 is not just about an old Cooper's hoop, but teases at how physical things can invoke history; #2 is not just a depiction of a broken chair, but a consideration of self-reflection and how we locate such activity in time ("how we were / or how we are now / or how we might yet be"); #3 considers the nature of pilgrimage, the spiritual versus the calculated and pre-defined route march; #4 uses an old spirit level - placed on an uneven surface - as a metaphor for the life balance we might seek individually, but which can be illusive; #5 is about language and the 'space' created by its absence, and uses the image of an Archaeologist to suggest how writers search for (then "clean", "polish" and "burnish") words - whilst underneath we are metaphorically still "scarred" individuals in shabby clothes.

The Refugee Dance

Whilst this poem is derived from eye-witness accounts of a specific refugee crisis, it is - in its brutality and the threat behind the smiling Captain and his gun - an image that can probably be applied to many such crises, especially where ethnic cleansing is an alleged factor. Are not all such 'political' situations laced with the potential for such violence?

The Search for Proof

Inspired by an article on the archaeological efforts to seek concrete evidence in relation to Jesus of Nazareth, this poem considers the relationship between the two, between physical proof and belief. The dichotomy is, if you will, between "the real man" and the 'unreal' man. "Shards" may be found, but they can only ever pertain to the former, never the latter. The piece strives for neutrality in terms of the Christian specific.

Theft

In the small chapel at Haddon Hall, just outside Bakewell in Derbyshire, there are some stained glass windows in which the Saints depicted now have plain empty faces, the originals having been removed in the 19th Century.

The Stone Circle

Exploring the relationship between the past and the present in a specific location, the poem holds up a mirror comparing the two. It does not attempt to judge between them, even if there is a hint of regret in the passing of time - though the dependence of the present on the past is clear.

End of an Ice Age

This is a picture of the present intruding on the past, and how modernity is most likely to trump tradition (it is based on Arctic Circle reindeer farmers).

The Catch

Cyclical changes in the natural world and specific eco-systems force people to adapt. For some of the fishermen in the poem the very word 'catch' takes on a different meaning.

Changing Faces

A collage piece - like "Punctuations from History" - borne out of a exhibition seen a number of years ago. The subject was 'Masks', primarily, but not exclusively, masks from the African continent. The titles of each of the eleven sections are taken from the titles of the masks chosen from the display. Much of the material is "found" from within the associated exhibition catalogue (now long since lost) and then subsequently manipulated and enhanced. There are a number of consistent themes running through the uses of the masks depicted, and therefore the individual pieces themselves: wealth, disguise, ceremony or ritual, the dead, expression, beauty etc.

Among the Ruins

I set out to create a poem with a simple metaphor: the parallel between a ruined old house and the broken down old man who once lived there as a child. Although there is a suggestion of a symbiosis here, the poem is really more about the affect of age on the man than the house; the physical collapse of the house akin to the need for a stick, his "hairless head".

Weather Forecast

Obviously this isn't a poem about the weather; the urgent wind is rather a cause of discomfort which, when allied with reflections triggered by a photograph, prompts a recollection of a meeting between the poet and another man. This other man is actually an earlier incarnation of the poet, in this instance a looking-forward man, not one looking backwards. Although he tried not to - still tries not too? - the poet loses this earlier version of himself. The piece is a somewhat melancholy consideration of how we are constantly 'losing' our 'younger selves' owing to the passage of time.

The Pennines - Early Winter

A more traditional piece inspired by one cold and frosty morning during a writing retreat at Garsdale in the Pennines. A little hackneyed perhaps, but when walking alone on the vastness of the moors your perspective shifts a little. There is a question here about what "influence" man - and his art - can truly have over the natural word.

Suburbia

There is a suggestion here that, while suburbia is traditionally regarded in a narrow and negative light, it may actually be something more positive in spite of its regimented uniformity.

Delta

The poem considers the relationship between land and water in a remote, undeveloped desert-like delta. The second stanza draws on an image of the human body.

Cocktails in the Infinity Pool

Singapore: a city that is all facade, depicting a shallow but conventional view of what we long for in our consumerist world? Possibly. But there is a past here too, where history struggles to find a voice or recognition.

Sandstorm

A light piece about the growth of a Near- or Middle-Eastern metropolis - and about the continuing influence of and dependence on the sea.

On Finding Themselves in Darkness

In a casual conversation, someone remarked on the beauty of the night sky. But this was in the light-polluted UK. Having experienced the night sky in a remote part of Africa, any sense of beauty and awe can be multiplied many-fold. Such an experience also focuses the mind on our insignificance in the cosmos.

Coast

"Coast" was partially inspired by the recent poems of Douglas Dunn (in "The Noise of a Fly") in which he often uses both 'lists' and rhyme. Although this piece didn't start out with much rhyme, some of the couplets begged for a more of a 'sing song' format, a playful tone supporting the sense of childhood nostalgia in the poem. It should be read aloud - and at some pace!

Islanders

We invest attributes and qualities in individuals who live particular lives - especially those whose existence we might regard as 'romantic'. They are not mythical beings of course, but subject to the same frailties as ourselves; only their frame of reference is different.

The Disenfranchised

An exploration as to how those more fortunate in society ("white-coated") perhaps distance themselves from the less fortunate ("The Disenfranchised") with a fabrication of concern that treats their subjects as little more than lab rats. The poem attempts to mirror that attitude by articulating the difficulties and deficiencies the disenfranchised face in their lives in a cool, detached manner.

The Psychologists

Prompted by some 'found' material on an entirely different subject, a poem that tries to depict the distance Psychologists are able to keep between themselves and their patients. There is ambiguity in the ending, however: are they dangerous because they get too close, or because they are responsible for altering lives without "the safety mark…in place"?

Making the Climb

An examination of the dichotomy between a traditional past and a modern, cosmopolitan present. From the perspective of the protagonist, it is the difference between passion and commitment, and a realm where no-one is an individual. The two interjections come one from each side of the divide.

Envy

There are always people we admire, look up to; people in whom we invest attributes they may or may not possess. If ever we truly recognise the impossibility of our being like them, or their failure to be as we imagine them, sometimes we metaphorically withdraw and allow that 'link' to wither.

Fragments

Three interwoven fragments, like strands in a plait. One shows the concrete; the second, a detached interpretation of such things; the final, a personal reflection itself fragmented by the vagaries of memory.

The Light of Our Lives

This is a piece about the loss of magic, particularly as it pertains to relationships. The 'fragment' is a metaphor, of course, an attempt to make tangible that which, for most people, usually defies description.

Sounds of the House

Starting out as an experiment based on the sounds one might inherit from immediate neighbour, this quickly became something with much more of a narrative about it. Using examples of what might be heard, it attempts to paint a picture of a man and his attitude towards his neighbour. Hopefully this can be read as loving / obsessive / caring / creepy etc. How one interprets it will be informed as much by the Reader themselves and their attitudes and predispositions as it will the bare words on the page.

Public Image

The intrusion that arises as a result of 'celebrity' is considered in this piece; the tendency of others to create a 'myth' of an individual for themselves - irrespective of the 'real' person. For the 'celebrity', it can be a negative experience that can compromise what they stand for - and leaves them longing for isolation and anonymity.

Fruit-crate Prophet and *Unearthing*

Two poems about searching for the "meaning for a life". Is such searching a little like alchemy i.e. something that is destined to remain profoundly unfulfilled? If so, and in the absence of any definitive answer, do we create personal and/or sociological 'meanings' to satisfy ourselves - and are these the "jewels" that need to be preserved? Sometimes our searching is for the unknowable or out of reach - a "common name" or "the mother lode of discovery". In any event, one needs to be persistent to try and decipher life, especially when so many are slavishly addicted to populist extremes. The final stanza - possibly in both poems - could be a sketching of the Writer's lot.

Ambition

The route to what we might regard as the end goal of our ambitions is beset by difficulties and traps (fog, gloom etc.). Certainty of what we want needs to be accompanied by passion and resoluteness.

Unauthorised Biography

What began as a piece about water in a landscape (now *Delta*) became a metaphor that suggested "rivers...that flow...through people's lives", and the notion of exploration seen as a parallel for biography. The sense here is not of 'approved' biography, but the kind of intrusive picking apart of celebrity for sensationalist ends.

Reflection in a Cracked Mirror

When you look in a cracked mirror, the image that is returned to you is fragmented, incoherent, and piecemeal. This poem attempts to reflect that discord to some extent, with the recognition of where we can find ourselves, "cast adrift from truth / in need of a chance to heal" - though it is debatable as to the long-term salving by "the looking back to see where we failed".

Lost

What is left when something goes away? Space. Nothingness. An intangible absence where that 'thing' once was. Often we try and re-create or re-live the past in an almost parasitic way; but where would we be if everyone did that? Such re-creation will inevitably be flawed; the past is just that. Is it better therefore, to keep what we have secure and private? If so, then what is the true role of poetry (or fiction, or autobiography) in terms of making the past 'live' again? And how successful can it really be? In the end, what is it that is 'Lost'; something we once had or ourselves?

The Wanting

The chicken-and-egg relationship of waiting and wanting is examined here. It is a kind of negative symbiotic relationship, with both elements forcing things upon us - inactivity, silence, motion, bullying - that generates an unresolvable perpetual dynamic.

Curse

What might a broken heart physically look like? What could it possibly still be good for other than motor function once it has been tortured, stamped on, tossed aside? Heart as 'poisoned entrails'.

Late to the Marquee

Using the image of a deserted and wind-ravaged marquee (for a wedding? a birthday? a christening?), a solitary poet sees it as a mirror for looking back on their "lost children" (i.e. things they may have written in the past of which no copies remain). This absence removes any possibility of celebration and therefore the purpose of the metaphorical tent, leaving the elements within it - such as ribbons and place cards - devoid of meaning.

Obsession

Simply the dangers that can arise from obsession, and the difficulty / impossibility of leaving it behind - or 'rewiring' ourselves ("a ham-fisted reboot").

Ninety-nine Percent

Recognising the potential to feel trapped by the 'daily grind', this offers a somewhat surreal picture of what 'freedom' might offer us: "large phone booths painted salmon pink". The poem suggests that even these bizarre symbols of 'freedom' are still likely to draw us back into the rules and mores from which we were trying to escape.

Greybeard's Lament

A tongue-in-cheek observation on the passing of time and how we feel that ageing only happens to others. The humour in the piece is offered by Doreen going about her duties, and the mysterious 'appearance' of Burt Lancaster, swashbuckling star of Hollywood 's Golden Era.

The Reticence of Evolution

The poem compares a kind of evolution with the imprisoned escaping over a boundary wall - but it is exploration that is fraught with difficulties, disappointments and profound failures. The intruding narrative (with a deliberate 'beat' to it) tries to juxtapose insights into what drives the explorers.

Slow-motion Apocalypse

It is intended that there is something 'other worldly' about the central images in this poem; if it gives the impression of being slightly 'trippy' or drug-induced, this is intentional. It posits the question as to what alternatives there may be to our "figurative existence" and what we might find there.

The Holly Leaf

A poem ignited by something as simple as a drive in the country and a reflection on how even the most mundane and ordinary of things - a dead leaf - can carry import for us.

Autumn

A single image of the absence of something expected - and the sense of disappointment when it isn't forthcoming.

Elemental

Starting out as an 'explorers poem' (akin to some pieces in "*Human Archaeology*"), the semi-found words distilled themselves into more or less discrete sections, and this allowed an exploration of a parallel with the mythical four elements (which also seemed to fit with the overall tone of the poem). Because Earth, Water, Air and Fire themselves would not perfectly align with the context of the work, the beginning of each stanza calls out the equivalences mapped. [If recited, the words in italics are not intended to be read aloud.]

Driving Home for Christmas

The core simile in this poem is that what we strive to communicate - for example in the inscriptions we write in Christmas cards - is like a fog i.e ultimately lacking clarity and definition no matter how hard we try (the "misplaced sense of security" we get from car headlights). Of course fog, in its infinite flexibility, can be a source of wonder and beauty too - something we would do well to remind ourselves, and to recognise the potential this offers us to "push on" in trying to communicate. Or, indeed, write poetry.

Trapped by the Tides

Simple enough: a poem inspired by a combination of an enormously clear harvest moon and insomnia!

Veritas

The poem suggests that, when people become drawn into the need to lie in order to satisfy a personal goal, it is not only truth that suffers. In the telling of lies, language itself is compromised. What effect does the corruption of language have on our ability to 'navigate'? And to tell the truth?

The Fallacy

In a way, this piece questions the value of 'Art'. It compares those who have failed - needing to resort to "hustling" and being subject to "the norm" - with those who believe they have succeeded somehow, and who have created a "stronghold" that is "nearly unbeatable". Of course there is no real difference between the two groups: "the Big Idea" remains, as it must, elusive and unaffected by our feeble attempts to tie it down.

Minutes

Time is more than a thief in this poem; it is a Trickster that both dupes and robs you.

www.ingramcontent.com/pod-product-compliance
Lightning Source LLC
Chambersburg PA
CBHW030530080526
44586CB00011B/390